Stars in the

Aurora Colón García

Rigby®

A Harcourt Achieve Imprint

www.Rigby.com
1-800-531-5015

Look up at the sky.
The sky at night is full of stars.
Stars are very far away.

Some stars are bright.
The North Star is a bright star.

Stars can be many colors.
Some stars are blue,
and some stars are white.
Some stars are yellow,
and some stars are red.

Our sun is a yellow star.

The sun is big,

but it looks small.

It's very far away.

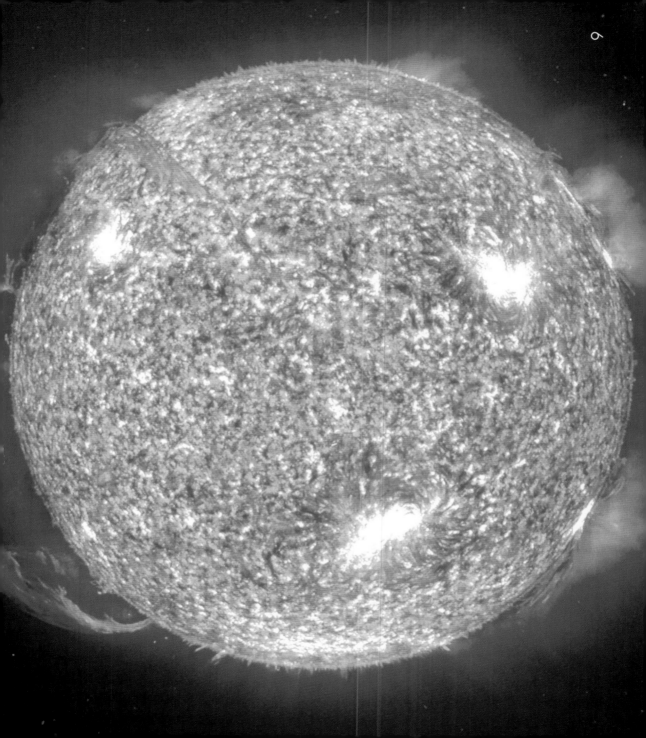

Sometimes groups of stars look like pictures. These stars look like a lion.

These stars look like a horse with wings.

These stars look like a saucepan.

You can make a star picture!
You need these things.

paper-towel tube

black paper

pencil

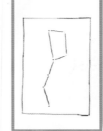
star picture

tape

scissors

1. Cut out a small circle from the black paper.

2. Copy the star picture onto the circle.

3. Tape the circle to one end of the tube.

4. Poke holes in the circle.

5. Hold up the tube to a light.

Look up at the sky.
What do you see?

The Materializer

By John Lockyer

Illustrated by Andrew Trimmer

Rigby

The Materializer

It was a shivery, sunless autumn afternoon. Rick knew he shouldn't have shot baskets after class. Now he was late for his job. Stopping outside the front gate of the old stone house, he was relieved to see there were no lights on inside. The Doctor wasn't home. He picked a key out of an empty clay pot on the porch and unlocked the front door.

Inference:

What inference can be made about how Rick feels about the Doctor?

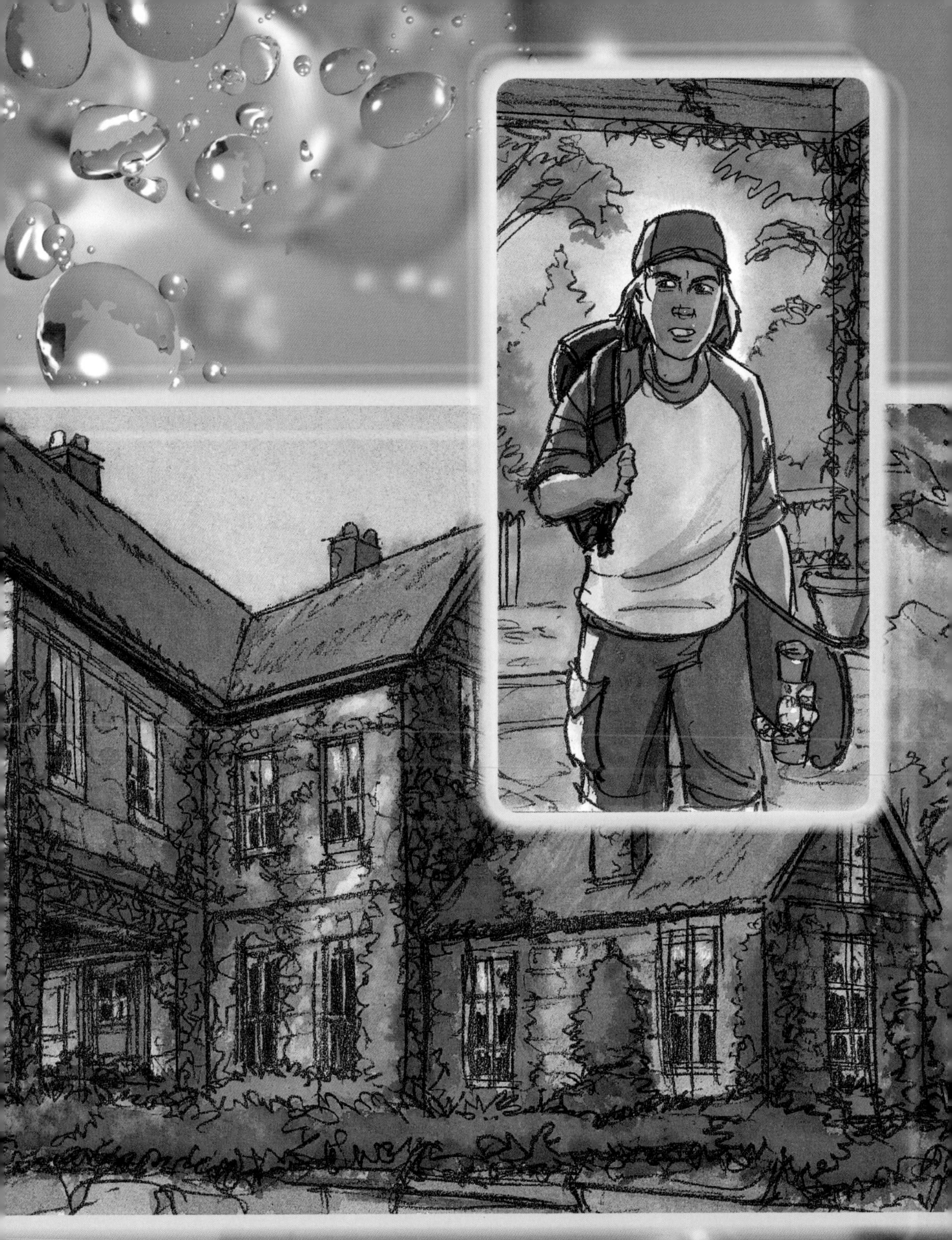

n inside

Inside, he hurried along the hallway and down to the basement. Fluorescent tubes flickered pale-blue light around the Doctor's laboratory.

Rick walked over to the benches where the Doctor stored his glassware — beakers, test tubes, vials, stirring rods — and checked them for cracks, smudges, and smears. With the broom, he did a quick once-around of the basement, flicking up bits of dust, grit, and chemical crystals.

In the center of the basement was a tall, square shape covered with black cloth. Rick didn't know what was underneath the cloth. He had never asked, and the Doctor had never told him.

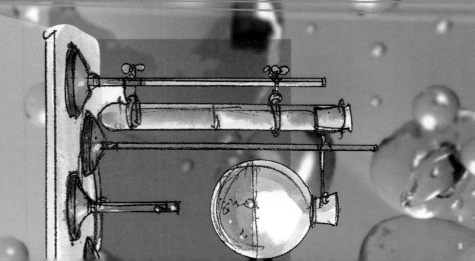

setting:

What words best describe the setting of the Doctor's laboratory?

cheerful   spooky   sunny   eerie   organized   chilling

fluorescent tubes flickered

As he dusted around it, he noticed a large spider's web fixed to one of the ceiling rafters. He grabbed a stool from under one of the benches, dragged it across the room, and climbed onto the top step.

The Doctor insisted he get rid of any small creatures in the laboratory. He said they could ruin years of research if they interfered with his experiments.

Rick could see the spider's thin black legs protruding from a crack in the ceiling. He reached out with a long duster, trying to sweep the web off the rafter. Stretching, he pushed up onto his toes.

question

How do you think spiders might ruin years of research?

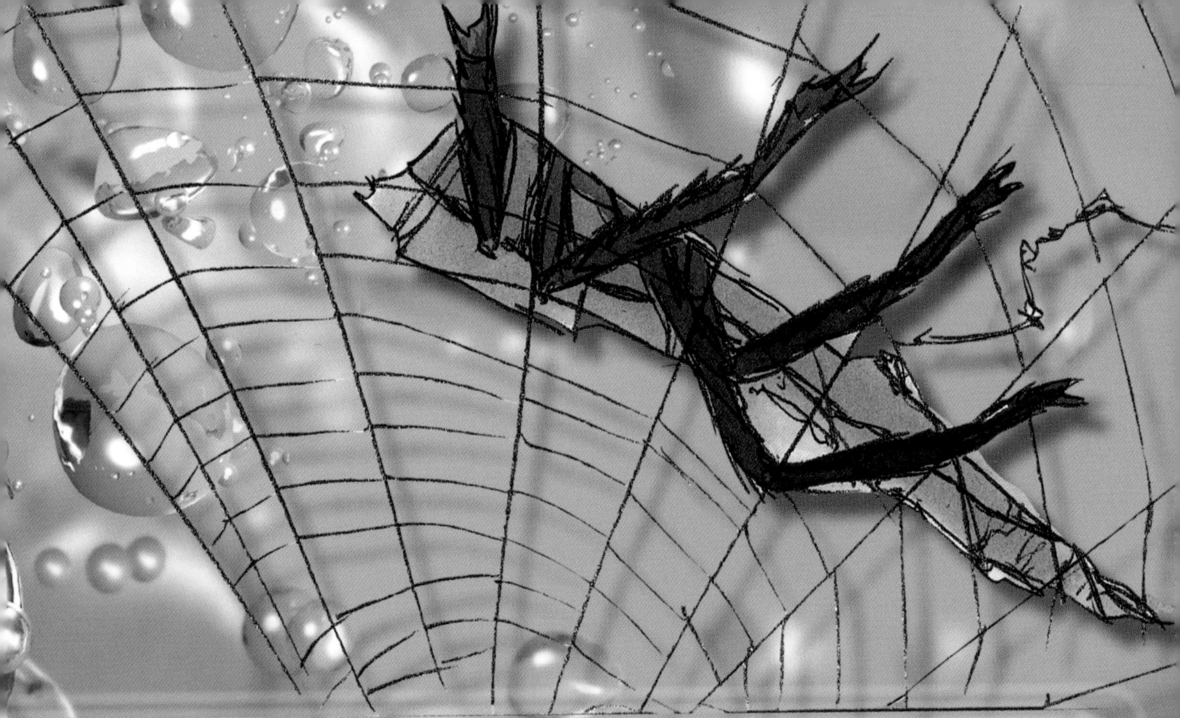

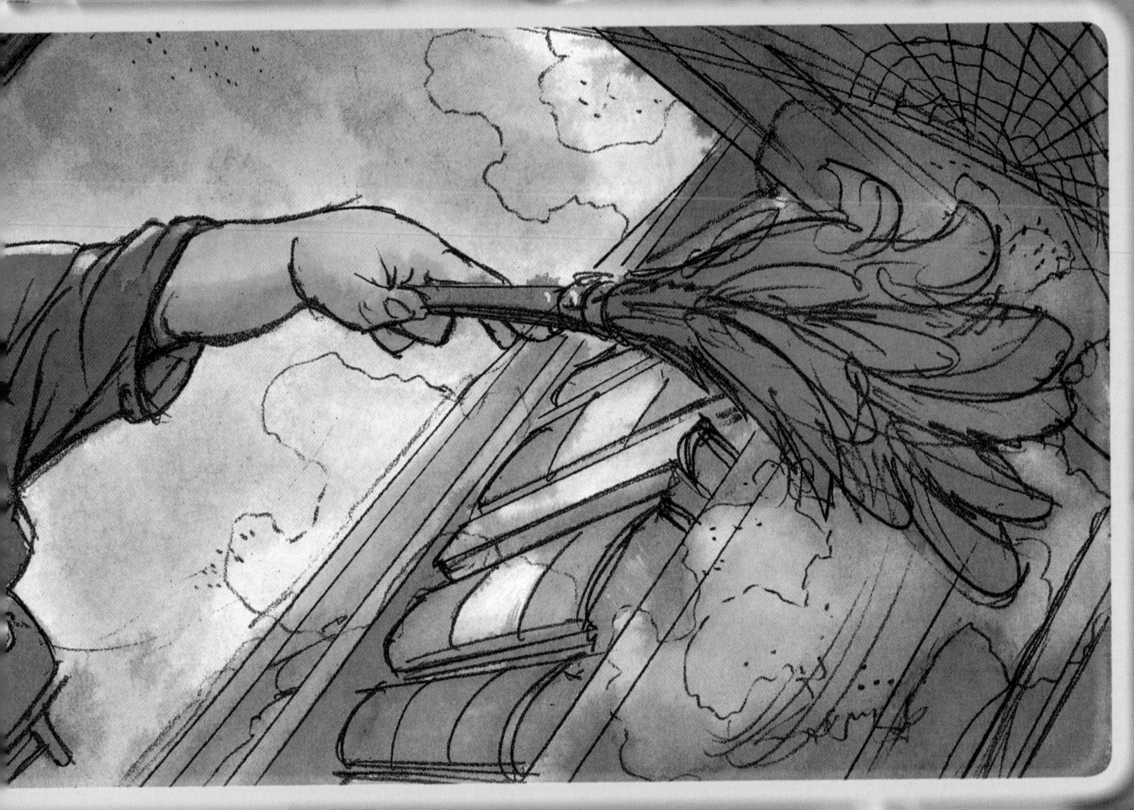

protruding

Suddenly the front door slammed shut, startling Rick. He teetered forward and dropped the duster. He snatched at the black cloth, trying to steady himself. The cloth ripped, sending him and the stool crashing to the floor.

As Rick got up, he saw the Doctor standing at the top of the stairs. His handlebar moustache twitched up and down. Rick scrambled to his feet.

"I . . . I was trying to . . ."

Predict:

What do you think
might happen
in the story now?

"... I was trying to ..."

The Doctor wasn't listening. He clomped down the stairs, his eyes fixed on the black-caped shape. He picked up the piece of torn cloth and stared at Rick. "If you have damaged this machine . . .," he hissed.

The Doctor bent down, gripped a corner of the black cloth, and tugged. The cloth slid off the shape, revealing two glass diamond shapes that dominated a huge machine. The diamonds were joined in the middle by a control panel.

Emotions

What words could describe the emotions Rick might be experiencing?

panic   excitement

fear   surprise   alarm

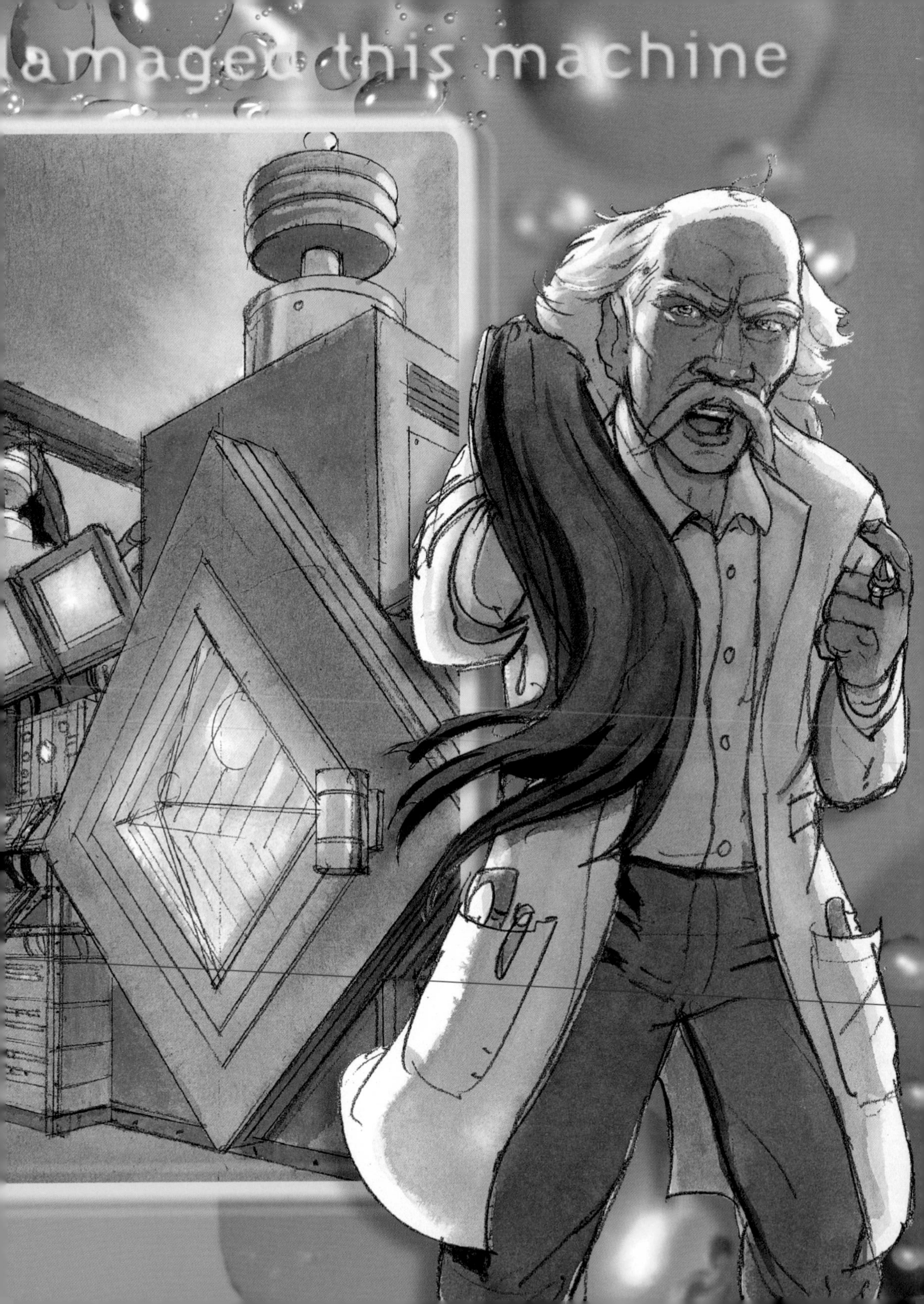
amaged this machine

Muttering to himself, the Doctor took a small wooden box from beneath the console, walked to the diamond on the right, and opened an almost invisible door. He placed the box on a metal disc in the diamond, closed the door, and returned to the console. He checked the settings of the dials and switches, then pressed a white button.

There was a faint fizzing sound. The space around the box turned bright yellow. The box glowed, too. Slowly it disintegrated, turning into hundreds of golden, spinning particles.

Clarify: console

a window

b a desk on which controls of an electronic device are mounted

c security panel

a, b, or c?

The particles spun faster and faster, bouncing off the walls. There was a sudden explosion of light. The particles formed into one beam. The beam fizzed out on the top of the machine, over the console, and into the other diamond. There the particles separated, settled on the disc, and slowly re-formed back into the box.

The Doctor lifted the box off the disc, turned it over in his hands, and grunted. "Everything appears undamaged."

Rick was fascinated. He edged closer to the machine. He stared from one diamond to the other. "How did that happen?"

The Doctor ignored his question.

Rick asked again. "How did you make the box move? Was it a magic trick?"

Action and Consequence:

ACTION	CONSEQUENCE
The particles spun faster and faster	The particles formed into one beam
The particles separated, settled on the disc, and	?

The Doctor spun around. "Magic!" he hissed. "You think I work in this basement day after day, conjuring up tricks?"

Rick shrugged, wishing he'd never asked.

The Doctor clenched his fists. "This machine is a materializer!" he shouted. "It transports objects through space!" He pointed at the box on the console, then turned to the right diamond and opened the door. "I place an object in here and center a powerful electrical field around it. The current is so strong, it transforms the object into a beam of moving particles. The beam is then directed to another location." He pointed to the other diamond. "When the electrical field switches off, the object re-forms itself — materializes. That's science, not magic."

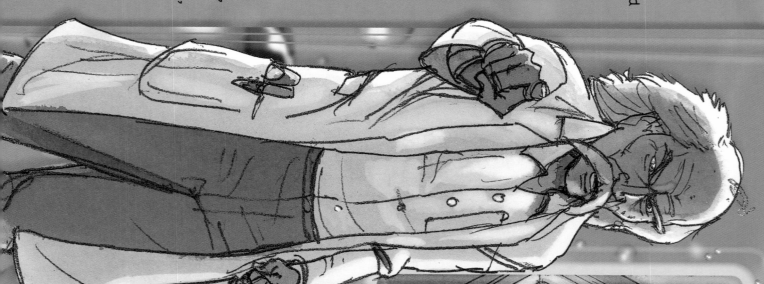

... that'

science not magic

Character Profile

What words might describe the character of the Doctor?

intelligent   impatient

kind   scary

interesting   friendly

intolerant   irritable

Rick decided it was a good time to leave. If he moved quietly, perhaps he wouldn't be noticed.

A movement on the rafter above the right diamond caught his eye as he sidled across the room. He stopped and looked up. The spider had come out of its crack. Trailing dewy silk, it flitted across the web's finely spun strands. When it reached the bottom of the web, it leaped, landing on the diamond. Sliding down the slippery surface, it came to rest on top of the door.

Clarify: sidled

a crept
b moved sneakily
c shuffled

a, b, or c?

Before Rick had a chance to say anything, the Doctor spun around.

"The materializer is not magic," he repeated angrily. "It is an extremely complex machine. It is designed to transport non-living and living things. In the future, there will be materializers in every building. Just by pressing a button, people will be able to instantly transport themselves to another building in any town, city, country, or continent. Imagine how that will change the way we live!"

He threw up his hands. "No more cars, buses, trains, ships, or aeroplanes . . . no more pollution."

He turned back to the console. "The test trials were finished yesterday. The materializer is now ready for transporting living things."

question:

What do you think could be a problem with having a materializer?

. . . no more pollution

While the Doctor was talking, the spider had slid down the door and scuttled inside the diamond. Rick pointed at the hairy creature. "Doctor!"

The Doctor glared at him. "Be silent! You have said too much already. Watch and you will see just how marvelous the materializer is!" He pressed the white button, hurried to the diamond, opened the door, stepped onto the disc, and pulled the door closed. The spider sat crouched in a corner behind him.

he pressec

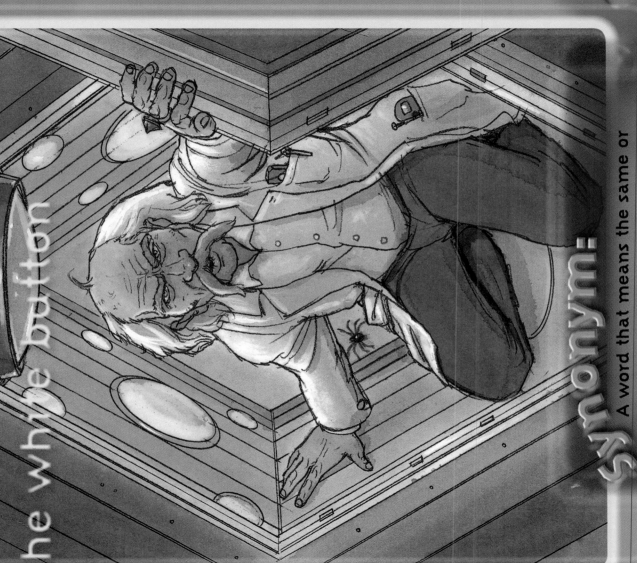

the white button

Synonym:

A word that means the same or nearly the same as another word.

What is the synonym for scuttled?

(a) ran around with short, hurried steps

(b) limped rapidly

a or b ?

Rick heard the faint fizzing sound. The space around the Doctor and the spider turned bright yellow. The Doctor and the spider glowed, too. Slowly they disintegrated, turning into thousands of golden, spinning particles. The particles spun faster and faster, bouncing off the walls and intermixing. There was a sudden explosion of light. The particles formed into one beam. The beam fizzed out of the top of the machine, over the console, and into the other diamond. There the particles separated and settled on the disc.

Clarify: disintegrated

a disappeared

b dissolved

c scattered

a, b, or c?

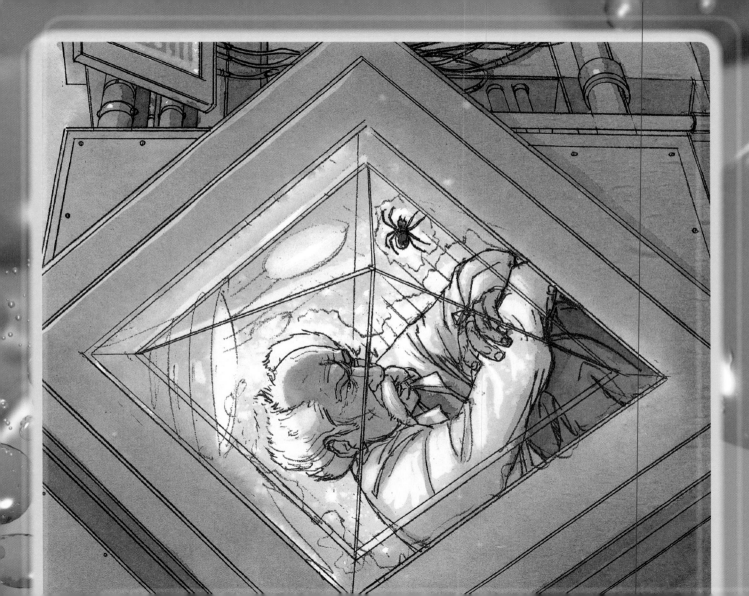

The spider formed first. It scuttled around the disc, raised its front legs onto the door, and pushed like it was trying to get out. One of its legs moved differently than the others. Rick kneeled down . . . the leg had a gold ring on it – just like the ring that the Doctor wore.

Trembling, Rick pushed himself away from the spider and ran. He slammed the front door behind him . . . and he knew that he would never return.

Summary

What main points would you put in a summary of *The Materializer*?

- Rick cleaned the Doctor's laboratory.

- The Doctor wasn't home.

- Rick noticed a spider on the ceiling.

- The Doctor insisted Rick get rid of small creatures.

- The Doctor thought Rick had damaged the materializer.

- The Doctor muttered to himself.

- The Doctor showed Rick what the materializer could do.

- The spider went inside the materializer.

- The spider and the Doctor disintegrated.

- A spider formed with a gold ring on its leg.

- Rick was terrified and ran out of the house.

What connections can you make to *The Materializer?*

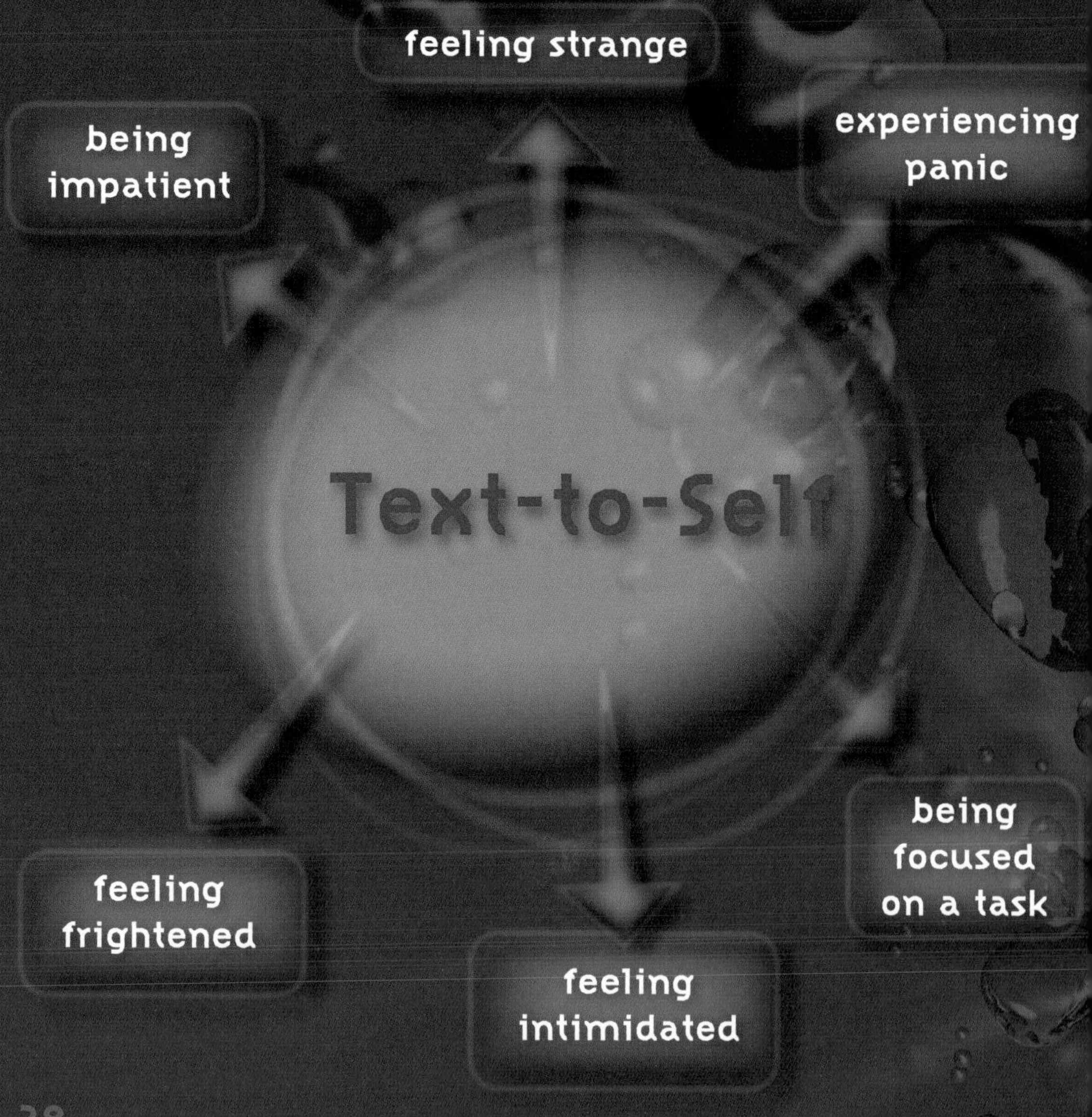

Text-to-Self

being impatient

feeling strange

experiencing panic

feeling frightened

feeling intimidated

being focused on a task

Text-to-Text

Talk about other texts you may have read that have similar features. Compare the texts.

Text-to-World

Talk about situations in the world that might connect to elements in the text.

Planning a Science Fiction Story

1 Decide on a storyline that has a problem and a resolution:

Rick works for a strange Doctor by cleaning his laboratory.

The Doctor is angry when Rick has accidentally uncovered his weird machine. The Doctor claims it can transport objects through space by disintegrating and reassembling them.

Rick wants to go, but the Doctor insists on demonstrating the machine. The Doctor claims it can transport objects through space by disintegrating and reassembling them.

Rick has to watch as the Doctor and an unseen spider enter the machine. They both disintegrate into spinning particles.

When the particles reassemble, the Doctor is gone, and only the spider remains, wearing the Doctor's ring.

2 Think about the characters:

Make some short notes or sketches.

Think about the way they think, act, and feel.

Rick

- polite
- curious
- lacking in confidence
- hard-working

the Doctor

- scary
- arrogant
- impatient
- intolerant
- demanding

3 Decide on the setting:

Old stone house with a basement laboratory that has eerie pale-blue lighting, and is cluttered with laboratory gear and a huge machine.

Science fiction stories usually feature . . .

- Scientific language and ideas

- Imaginary or futuristic worlds

- A fear of the unknown

- A sense of being alien in a strange environment

- Things that are not as they appear to be